FANTASTIC FORCES

Air and Water Pressure

Richard Spilsbury

Heinemann
LIBRARY

www.heinemann.co.uk/library
Visit our website to find out more information about Heinemann Library books.

To order:
 Phone 44 (0) 1865 888066
 Send a fax to 44 (0) 1865 314091
 Visit the Heinemann Bookshop at www.heinemann.co.uk/library to browse our catalogue and order online.

First published in Great Britain by
Heinemann Library, Halley Court, Jordan Hill,
Oxford, OX2 8EJ, part of Harcourt Education.

Heinemann Library is a registered trademark
of Harcourt Education Ltd.

Editorial: Nancy Dickmann and Catherine Veitch
Design: Richard Parker and Tinstar Design
    (www.tinstar.co.uk)
Picture Research: Erica Newbery and Susi Paz
Production: Camilla Crask
Index: Indexing Specialists (UK) Ltd

Originated by Modern Age
Printed and bound in China by WKT
  Company Limited

13-digit ISBN: 978 0 431 18040 3
11 10 09 08 07
10 9 8 7 6 5 4 3 2 1

British Library Cataloguing in Publication Data

Spilsbury, Richard, 1963-
Air and water pressure. - (Fantastic forces)
551.5'4
A full catalogue record for this book is available
from the British Library.

Acknowledgements
The publishers would like to thank the following
for permission to reproduce photographs:
Alamy pp. **5** (Aflo Foto Agency), **6** (The
Photolibrary Wales), **7** (Bryan & Cherry Alexander
Photography), **12** (Gavin Hellier), **14** (Chris
Sattlberger), **16** (Jochen Tack); Corbis pp. **24**
(Steve Kaufman), **18, 19**; Getty Images pp. **4,
9, 23** (Photodisc), **11** (Carsten Peter/National
Geographic), **17** (Brand X Pictures), **22**
(National Geographic/Darlyne A Murawski);
Harcourt Education pp. **10, 13, 20, 25** (Tudor
Photography); www.internationalrobotics.com
p. **27**; Tony Dillon p. **26**.

Cover photograph of reproduced with permission
of Getty Images/The Image Bank/Zac Macaulay.

Every effort has been made to contact copyright
holders of any material reproduced in this book.
Any omissions will be rectified in subsequent
printings if notice is given to the publishers.

Disclaimer

Contents

Any words appearing in the text in bold,
like this, are explained in the glossary.

Air and water pressure experiments and demonstrations

There are several experiments and demonstrations in this book that will help you to understand how air and water pressure work. Each experiment or demonstration contains a list of the equipment you need and step-by-step instructions. You should ask an adult to help you with any sharp objects.

Materials you will use

Most of the experiments and demonstrations in this book can be done with household objects that can be found in your own home. You will also need a pencil and paper to record your results.

What is pressure?

When you push a doorbell the **pressure** from your finger makes an electric chime work. Pressure is a **force** pressing against something. Pressure changes depending on the size of area it presses on.

A force is a push or pull. Although you cannot see a force you can usually see what it does to an object. Some forces change the shape or size of an object. A rubber band stretches when you pull on either end of it. A drink can crumples when you squeeze it.

Some forces make things move or change the speed at which they move. For example, a tennis player serves by throwing the ball into the air slowly and then hitting it hard with their racket. This makes the ball move fast over the net. Other forces can change the direction of something that is already moving. See what happens in a game of marbles when the moving balls bash into each other.

A rubber will not work unless you use pressure to press it against the paper.

The force of the racket strings hits a small area of the tennis ball. It pushes the elastic inside the ball together. The ball then springs away from the racket.

When a force presses on a small area, it presses very hard. The pressure is high. Try pushing your finger into a cork pinboard. Your fingertip cannot do more than make a dent in the pinboard. Now try pushing a drawing pin into the same pinboard using the same force. You will find that you can push it in easily. The reason is that all the force of your push was touching the pinboard at the tiny, sharp tip of the pin, rather than across the whole of the end of your finger. The pressure at the pin tip is higher than the pressure under your fingertip.

5

Scrap cars are crushed into small blocks of metal using presses. The presses apply massive forces to small areas. This creates high pressure.

How do we measure pressure?

We measure pressure by measuring the amount of force that presses on a particular area. Forces are measured in **newtons** (N). One newton is about the amount of force it would take to lift an apple. Pressure, or the amount of force pressing on an area, is measured in pascals (Pa).

Have a look at the table opposite. It compares the pressure on the ice made by an ice skater with and without skates. The force on the ice stays the same. This is because the skater is the same **mass** on the ice whether they wear their skates or carry their skates. However, the pressure on the ice changes.

This is because different size areas press on the ice. The blade of one ice skate is a smaller area than the blades of two ice skates. The pressure from one ice skate is much higher than the pressure from two ice skates. The smaller the area is, the greater the pressure.

	Mass (kilograms)	Force (newtons)	Area in sq. m (sq. ft)	Pressure (pascals)
Ice skater standing on ice holding skates	65	650	0.05 (0.5)	12,800
Ice skater standing on a pair of skates	65	650	0.0004 (0.004)	1,625,000
Ice skater balancing on one skate	65	650	0.0002 (0.002)	3,250,000

The person walking across the snow does not sink because he spreads the force of his weight over the large area of the snowshoes. The pressure on the snow is less.

7

What is air pressure?

Things on Earth are **solids**, **liquids**, or **gases**. Air is made up of a mixture of gases. The gases in air contain billions of tiny **particles** called **molecules**.

Air molecules bounce off things and against each other, rather like rubber balls. They push against surfaces all around them. This is what we call **air pressure**.

Moving air molecules press against and bounce off every surface. Real air molecules are tiny and invisible!

Earth's atmosphere is about 560 km (348 miles) thick. The clouds we see from space are part of the atmosphere.

What is atmospheric pressure?

Between the Earth's surface and space there is a layer of air called the **atmosphere**. The atmosphere contains thousands of tonnes of air molecules. The **force** of Earth's **gravity** pulls the molecules in Earth's atmosphere downwards. The weight of all that air presses down on everything on our planet. This **pressure** is called **atmospheric pressure**.

Does atmospheric pressure squash me?

Atmospheric pressure does not squash us because we have air inside our bodies, too. Air is tucked away in lots of places such as in our **lungs**, between our **cells**, and in our ears. This air is pressing out on our bodies from the inside. This outward force balances the inward force of the atmosphere.

DEMONSTRATION:

Heavy air

Air has weight, so a blown-up balloon will weigh more than an empty one.

Equipment: Two identical balloons, a straight stick or a ruler about 100 cm (39 inches) long, string, a needle.

Demonstration steps:

1. Blow up both balloons full of air. Remember, take breaks between blows and pinch the end of the balloon to stop the air escaping!
2. Once the balloons are full, tie the ends.
3. Tie a balloon to each end of the stick.
4. Hang up or hold the stick from the middle. The stick should balance because an equal weight of air hangs in the balloon on each end.
5. Now carefully pop one balloon with the needle. What happens?

Explanation: When you pop one balloon the blown-up balloon pulls down on the stick. The blown-up balloon pulls down on the stick because it contains air and so it weighs more. The air escapes from the popped balloon so it is lighter.

When does atmospheric pressure change?

Imagine a pile of books stacked from floor to ceiling. If you were the book at the bottom, you would have more **force** pressing on you than if you were a book halfway up the pile. It is the same with **atmospheric pressure**. It changes depending on how high up you are above the Earth's surface.

On land

On the ground, at **sea level**, all of the **atmosphere** is pressing down on you. The atmospheric pressure is high. High up in the mountains, at high **altitude**, not so much of the atmosphere is pressing down on you. The atmospheric pressure is low.

In space

When you go above the Earth's atmosphere into space there is almost no air. Air **molecules** are so widely spaced that they make no **air pressure**. A place with no air pressure is called a **vacuum**.

DID YOU KNOW?

Air at high altitude is often described as thin because the air molecules are spread apart. The air has low **pressure**. You need to breathe faster to get enough **oxygen** molecules from the thin air.

Most mountain climbers wear oxygen masks when climbing very high mountains. The air is too thin for them to breathe.

High air pressure usually gives fine, clear weather. Low pressure usually means the weather will be unsettled. It might be wet and windy.

How does air pressure affect weather?

Heat from the Sun warms the air above the Earth unevenly. Heated air molecules move quicker and bounce about more than cold molecules. This makes warm air lighter than cold air because the molecules are not so closely packed together. When something is lighter than something else, but takes up the same space, it is less **dense**.

Warm air is less dense and rises through the atmosphere. This leaves gaps with fewer air molecules and low atmospheric pressure. Colder air moves into these low-pressure gaps. These air movements create winds. Winds blow rain clouds into the gaps, causing wet weather. High atmospheric pressure is caused by sinking, denser cold air. Weather is drier because winds blow clouds away. We use an instrument called a **barometer** to measure air pressure and predict how the weather will change.

EXPERIMENT:

Make a simple barometer

Question: Does atmospheric pressure affect water level?

Hypothesis: As the atmospheric pressure in the air increases, it will push down on the surface of the water in the glass. This will make the level of water rise *inside* the bottle. As the atmospheric pressure in the air decreases, it will not push down so hard on the surface of the water. This will make the level of water lower *inside* the bottle.

Equipment: Transparent glass or jug, small empty transparent bottle, marker pen.

Experiment steps:
1. Fill the glass halfway up with water.
2. Turn the empty drink bottle upside down into the glass. Add more water if the top of the water is not in the widest part of the bottle.
3. Use the marker pen to draw a line on the glass to show the water level.
4. Check the glass after a few days. Has the level changed?

Conclusion: Changes in air pressure can be seen in a water barometer. When the air pressure is high, it presses more on the water in the glass and this raises the water level inside the bottle. When the air pressure is lower, the water level is lower too.

How do we use air pressure?

Air pressure makes games such as basketball fun! Air **molecules** are pumped inside the **inflated** balls. The air pressure is high because lots of air molecules are squashed inside the ball. The **force** of the ground hitting the ball scatters the air molecules inside the ball. This releases energy. The energy makes the ball bounce. The lower the air pressure in the ball, the less it bounces.

Tyres and airbags

Have you ever ridden a bike with a flat tyre? You feel a bump as you ride over a stone. This is the force of the stone against a small area on the hard wheel. With inflated tyres, air pressure spreads the force all around the hard wheel, so you feel it less.

Heavy trucks don't get stuck in mud because air pressure spreads their weight across many large tyres.

air pushes
up drink

air

How does air pressure help you suck up a drink through a straw? You suck by lowering the air pressure in your mouth. The only way air can get in to balance pressures is through the straw. Your drink is in the way so the air pushes it out of the way to get into your mouth.

In a car crash airbags inflate to increase the area a passenger hits. This means the impact force of the car creates less **pressure** on the passenger's body. Pressure over a large area is much smaller than pressure over a small area.

Breathing and suction

When you open a valve on a bike tyre, you hear some high-pressure air hissing out. It moves fast into the lower-pressure air outside because different air pressures always try to balance out. We rely on this for breathing. Your **lungs** expand when you breathe in. The air molecules inside your lungs spread out. This lowers the air pressure inside your lungs. Air outside your body rushes into the lungs through your nose and mouth. You breathe out when your lungs are squeezed smaller. The air pressure inside your lungs increases. Air is forced out of your lungs.

15

Suction machines

Vacuum cleaners have an electric pump that removes air from inside the machine. This creates a **vacuum**, with no air. The only way higher-pressure air from outside can get into this vacuum is through a tube. Air from outside is sucked in through the tube. The air carries with it light dirt and dust from the ground.

The sucker on a toy dart sticks to smooth surfaces. When you press the sucker against a surface, the air inside the cup gets squeezed out. This creates a vacuum, so the air pressure outside the cup is higher. It presses the cup against the surface.

DID YOU KNOW?

Otto von Guericke demonstrated the power of suction in the 1600s. He made two metal ball halves and sucked out the air from between them. **Atmospheric pressure** pushed the ball halves together, even when two teams of horses tried to pull them apart.

We use air pressure to remove dust and dirt from our homes using vacuum cleaners.

Skydiving

Anything in the air is pulled down towards the Earth by a force called **gravity**. Skydivers use parachutes to stop them hurting themselves when they land after jumping from aeroplanes. A parachute is shaped like an upside down bowl. It traps the air molecules underneath it and squashes them together. The air molecules push up against the parachute. This push is a force called **air resistance**. It slows the skydiver down.

Staying in the air

To stay in the air, people must balance the upward push of air resistance with the downward force of gravity. Hot air balloons stay in the air using a gigantic bag of warmed air. Warm air in the balloon is less **dense** than the air around it, so the balloon rises. Hot air balloon pilots use burners to warm up the air inside the balloon when it starts to cool.

At a balloon rally, you can hear the roar of burners as pilots heat the air inside their balloons.

What is water pressure?

In the bath you can feel the water pressing gently on your body. Like air, water is also made up of **molecules**. The molecules are heavier and more **densely** packed together than the molecules in air. That is why we can see and feel water, but not air. **Water pressure** is the pushing effect of water molecules against surfaces in and around it.

An easy way to see water pressure at work is in a hosepipe. Hosepipes are floppy and flat when there is no water in them. But they become hard and rounded when the tap is switched on. Water pressure pushes out the sides as far as they can go. It is rather like the way a bouncy castle stands up when air is put into it.

Firefighters use water pressure to force water onto fires from a safe distance away.

Water pressure pushes against this diver from all directions. It presses the mask against his face.

Changing water pressure

When you get into a swimming pool you do not feel water pressure at first. But if you put on some goggles and dive, or stick your head underwater you can feel the goggles press harder around your eyes. That is because water pressure increases with depth. The deeper you go, the greater the amount of water molecules pushing down on you. The weight of water pushes the water molecules close together. The water pressure is high.

Popping ears

You may feel your ears pop underwater if you swallow. The popping is the sound of air rushing through your ears as the **pressure** changes in your ears.

EXPERIMENT:

Squirting carton

Question: Does water pressure increase with depth?

Hypothesis: The water will travel the furthest from the bottom hole, as the pressure is greatest here.

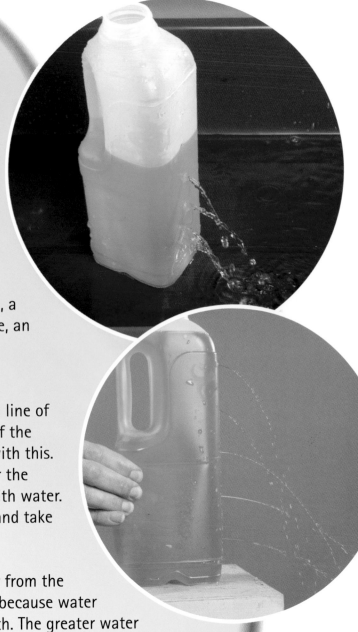

Equipment:
1 litre (2 pint) empty milk carton, a deep tray, a large nail, sticky tape, an adult to help.

Experiment steps:
1. Use a nail to carefully pierce a line of holes evenly down the front of the carton. Ask an adult to help with this.
2. Stick a long piece of tape over the holes and fill up the carton with water.
3. Stand the carton on the tray and take off the tape.

Conclusion: Water flows further from the bottom holes than the top ones because water pressure does increase with depth. The greater water pressure near the bottom of the carton gives the water a bigger push out of the hole.

What is pressure like in oceans?

Over three-quarters of the Earth's surface is covered with seawater, mostly about 1 kilometre (half a mile) deep. The deepest parts of the oceans are over 11 kilometres (7 miles) deep. That is as deep below **sea level** as the top of Mount Everest is above sea level. The **water pressure** at this depth is 1,000 times greater than at the surface.

Diving deep

As you go deeper, the water pressure can harm or even crush your body. Divers carry tanks of air to breathe when they dive underwater. Below 30 metres (98 feet) it is very difficult for divers to breathe normally because the pressure squashes their **lungs**.

At the ocean surface water pressure equals **atmospheric pressure**. For each 100 metres (330 feet) of depth, water pressure becomes ten times greater than **air pressure**.

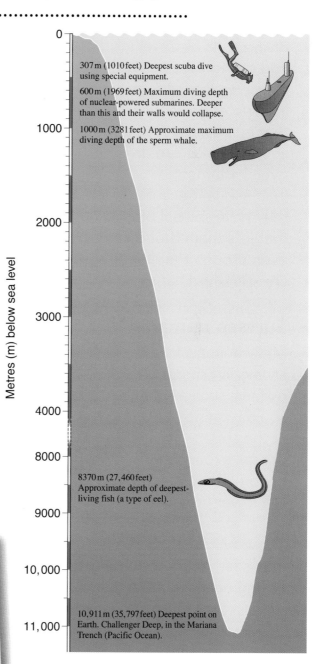

307 m (1010 feet) Deepest scuba dive using special equipment.

600 m (1969 feet) Maximum diving depth of nuclear-powered submarines. Deeper than this and their walls would collapse.

1000 m (3281 feet) Approximate maximum diving depth of the sperm whale.

8370 m (27,460 feet) Approximate depth of deepest-living fish (a type of eel).

10,911 m (35,797 feet) Deepest point on Earth. Challenger Deep, in the Mariana Trench (Pacific Ocean).

Metres (m) below sea level

0
1000
2000
3000
4000
8000
9000
10,000
11,000

Humans can dive much deeper if they protect themselves from the high **pressures** underwater. They wear special diving suits or travel inside submarines and diving capsules with strong walls. However, lots of sea animals can dive into water pressures 100 times those that humans can cope with. For example, sperm whales can dive over 1 kilometre (half a mile) because they have special blood that lets them breathe even though their lungs are squashed flat.

Surface damage

Many animals that always live in deep oceans, such as giant squids, cannot survive at the surface. Their organs expand and become damaged in the lower pressure water at the surface. These animals are usually only seen dead when deep fishing nets catch them.

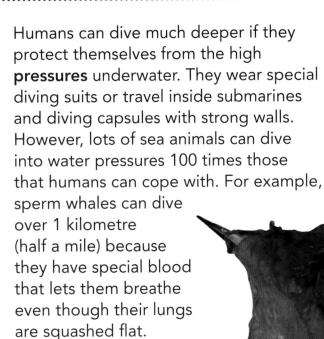

This deep-sea anglerfish survives in much deeper water than most sea animals. But it would not survive at the surface.

Why do things float or sink?

If you drop a coin in water it will sink, but an enormous steel ship that weighs much more than the coin will float. This is because of **buoyancy**.

How does buoyancy work?

Buoyancy means how well an object floats. It depends on the size of two **forces**: **gravity** and **upthrust**. Gravity pulls things down, while upthrust pushes them up.

Upthrust is the force of water pushing up against an object. The amount of upthrust on an object is the same as the weight of water it pushes aside or **displaces**. The bigger things are, the more water they displace and the harder the water pushes back on them. A big ship displaces more water than a coin. There is more upthrust pushing back against it to keep it afloat.

Any boat floats if the force of upthrust is greater than the downwards force of gravity pulling on it.

upthrust

gravity

Submarines use **ballast tanks** with air inside to control the depth they float at under water. They replace some of the air with heavy seawater to sink.

Controlling buoyancy

All ships need to be at the right level in the water. If they are too high in the water, they may be pushed over by waves and winds. Oil tankers are giant ships that transport heavy oil across the oceans. When the tanker has unloaded its oil, it is much lighter. The crew fills the empty spaces with seawater so that the tanker is not too light. Divers who need to work underwater put on weighted belts. They can add or take away weights to control their buoyancy.

DID YOU KNOW?

The *Knock Nevis* is the biggest oil tanker in the world. It is the same area as 161 tennis courts and weighs more than 1,350 jumbo jets! When full of oil, the supertanker sinks 26 metres (85 feet) beneath the waves. When it is empty, the *Knock Nevis* is too buoyant to remain stable.

EXPERIMENT:

Diving ballpoint pen top

Question: Can the buoyancy of an object be changed?

Hypothesis: The buoyancy of an object can be increased or decreased by changing the **air pressure** inside it.

Equipment: A pen top, a small lump of modelling clay, a tall glass of water, a transparent plastic bottle with screw-on cap.

Experiment steps:

1. If your pen top has a hole in the top, plug it with a small blob of modelling clay.
2. Squeeze modelling clay around the tail end of the pen top.
3. Place the pen top in the glass of water, with the tail end pointing down. Add or remove clay until it floats with its top sticking out of the water. The pen top is your diver.
4. Fill the bottle almost to the top with water. Fill slowly to avoid extra bubbles.
5. Put the diver in the bottle and screw on the cap.
6. Squeeze the bottle. What happens to the diver? Let go. What happens to the diver now?

Conclusion: When you squeeze the bottle, you increase the **water pressure** inside. This pushes water into the diver, squashing the air into a smaller space and making the diver sink. When you release the bottle, the air inside the diver expands and pushes water out. This increases buoyancy, so the diver rises.

25

How do we use water pressure?

What do water pistols, fountains, and power washers have in common? They all shoot out water by pushing it through small holes. **Pressure** increases when it acts on a smaller area. Shooting water through small holes increases its pressure. We use the power of high-pressure water in many different ways.

Increasing pressure

Electric pumps are used to get water into our homes from the **reservoir** pools where it is stored. The pump pushes water through pipes to our homes. The water is stored in tanks at the top of our homes. The **force** of **gravity** pushes the water down pipes to our taps.

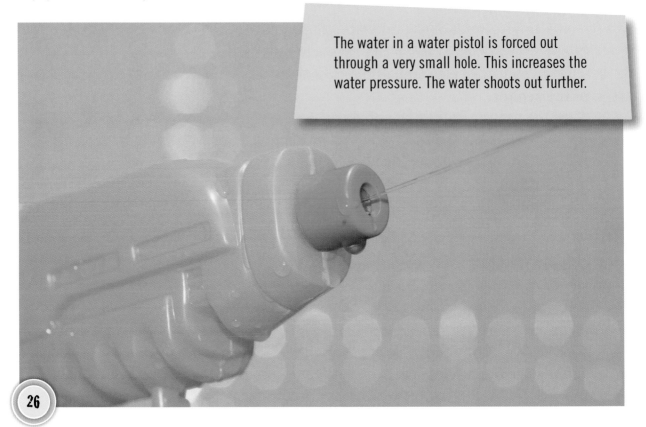

The water in a water pistol is forced out through a very small hole. This increases the water pressure. The water shoots out further.

Powerful water pistols

In powerful water pistols, water is sucked into a balloon. As the balloon fills, its elastic walls push on the water inside it. This increases the **water pressure** in the balloon. Water shoots out when you release a trigger.

Water pistons

Water pressure can be used to operate machines. **Jacks** are machines that lift heavy weights, such as cars. They have two cylinders, one narrow and one wide, connected together by a pipe. The cylinders and pipe are filled with water. Inside each cylinder is a plunger called a **piston**.

By pushing the pistons up and down, water is squeezed through the cylinders and pipes. This increases the pressure of the water.

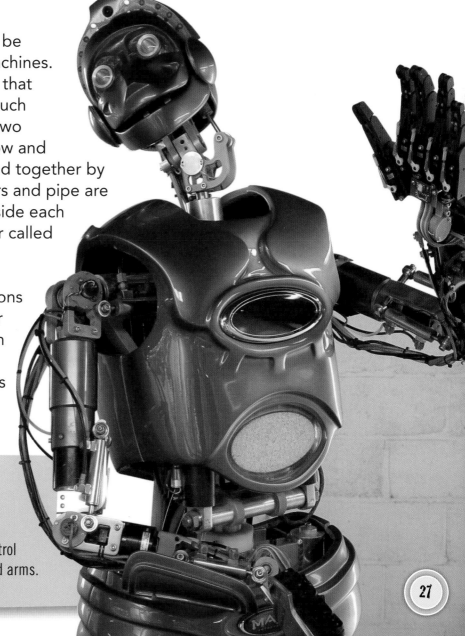

This AnthroBot is a type of robot that uses water pressure. Small water pistons inside control movement of its legs and arms.

27

People who found
the answers

Archimedes (about 287–212 B.C.)

Archimedes was a mathematician in Ancient Greece. His king wanted to know if his crown was pure gold. Archimedes realized that if cheaper metal was mixed with gold, the crown would be a different weight. It would **displace** a different amount of water from the same weight of pure gold. Archimedes discovered this after taking a bath. He saw that he displaced water. By measuring the amount of water his body displaced he could work out its **volume**. Archimedes ran outside shouting "Eureka" (which means "I have found it"). The crown displaced more water than pure gold. The crown was not pure gold.

Thomas Newcomen (1663–1729)

Newcomen was an English engineer who invented a pump engine. It worked using **atmospheric pressure** to push on a **piston** and suck up water. His invention was used to remove water from coal mines deep under ground. It helped prevent flooding and saved many miners' lives.

Auguste Piccard (1884–1962)

Piccard was an inventor and explorer. In 1931, he flew a balloon 15.8 kilometres (51,961 feet) into the **atmosphere**, higher than ever before. He survived the low atmospheric pressure, which could damage his body, in a special metal ball. In 1947, Piccard built a similar sphere to survive high **water pressure**. In 1960, his son Jacques piloted this machine over 10 kilometres (6 miles) under the ocean.

Amazing facts

- ## Lowest air pressure

  Have you heard of the eye of a hurricane? It is the calm bit in the middle that violent winds blow around. In 2005 scientists measured **air pressure** in the eye of Hurricane Wilma. It was about one-fifth lower than any other ever recorded on Earth.

- ## Different plimsoll lines

  Plimsoll lines are painted on ships to make sure they float safely at the right height in the water. This stops them being heavier or lighter than they should be. Ships with the same load need to use higher plimsoll lines when they move from seawater to freshwater. This is because freshwater is less **dense**, so the ships sink a little deeper.

- ## Powerful pump

  The space shuttle runs on **liquid** hydrogen fuel. Its engines need to produce lots of power to get it into space, so it has strong pumps to squirt the fuel in fast. The pumps are so powerful they could send a column of fuel 57 kilometres (36 miles) into the air!

- ## The *Trieste*

  The deepest diving machine ever built was the *Trieste*. It weighed 13 tonnes (14.3 tons) in air, but only 8 tonnes (8.8 tons) in sea water because of its **buoyancy**. The pilots were sealed in a 2-metre (6-feet) metal sphere with 12.7 centimetre (5 inch) thick walls to withstand the high water pressure over 10 kilometres (6 miles) underwater.

- ## Riding on air

  Hovercrafts are machines that move over water or land on a cushion of air. Giant fans blow air downwards into a space beneath the vehicle. This creates high air pressure that pushes the hovercraft off the surface it is travelling over.

Glossary

air pressure air molecules bouncing against each other and other objects

air resistance pushing force of air molecules against a moving object

altitude height above sea level

atmosphere air surrounding Earth

atmospheric pressure pressure of the atmosphere on Earth's surface

ballast tank compartment in a ship or submarine that is filled with seawater to control buoyancy

barometer instrument for measuring atmospheric pressure

buoyancy ability of an object to float in air or water

cell basic building block of all living things

dense tightly packed together

displace push aside. Any floating object displaces an equal weight of water.

force push or pull that makes an object move, speed up, change direction, or slow down

gas substance with widely spaced molecules that can expand to fill the space it is in

gravity force that pulls all objects towards the centre of Earth

inflated filled with air

jack machine that lifts a heavy weight. It is powered by a water piston.

liquid substance that flows and always has the same volume

lungs organs in the body used to breathe oxygen from air

mass amount of matter that an object contains. Mass causes objects to have weight.

molecule tiny amount of a substance

newton unit that measures a force. One newton is the force needed to lift an apple.

oxygen gas in air that we breathe in

particle a very small piece of material

piston plunger in a cylinder that moves up and down

pressure force pressing against something

reservoir large artificial lake

sea level average height of the surface of the oceans

solid substance of definite shape and volume made up of closely packed molecules

Glossary

upthrust force that pushes up. It acts in the opposite direction to gravity.

vacuum space with no air or air pressure

volume space occupied by something

water pressure pushing force of water molecules on objects

Further information

Books

Measuring the Weather: Wind and Air Pressure, Alan Rodgers and Angella Streluk (Heinemann Library, 2003)

Science Experiments: Water, Sally Nankivell-Aston and Dot Jackson (Franklin Watts, 2003)

Solids, Liquids and Gases, Rebecca Hunter (Franklin Watts, 2003)

Tabletop Scientist: Air. Steve Parker (Heinemann Library, 2005)

Websites

There are some fun activities and information about air pressure at *http://kids.earth.nasa.gov/archive/air_pressure/index.html*

Find out more about wind and air pressure at: *http://www.bwea.com/edu/wind.html*

Index

Titles in the *Fantastic Forces* series include:

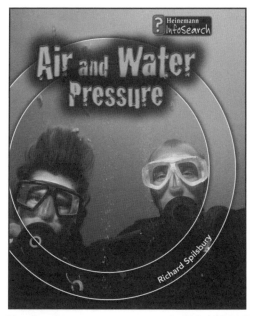

Hardback: 0 431 180407

Hardback: 0 431 180415

Hardback: 0 431 180423

Hardback: 0 431 180431

Find out about other titles from Heinemann Library on our website www.heinemann.co.uk/library